Original title:
The Sea's Ancient Memory

Copyright © 2025 Creative Arts Management OÜ
All rights reserved.

Author: Jasper Montgomery
ISBN HARDBACK: 978-1-80587-285-6
ISBN PAPERBACK: 978-1-80587-755-4

Treasures of the Timeless Depths

Bubbles rise, treasure lies,
A crab with hues, oh what a surprise!
Gold doubloons, they have no claims,
Just a fish playing silly games.

A sock from someone long ago,
Swimming here with quite the flow.
Nautical jokes from sea turtles roll,
Laughing waves with a salty soul.

Fathoms of the Past

In a boot where a fish once slept,
Old jellys are secrets that wept.
An anchor's dance, a buoy's sway,
Making friends, come what may.

Starfish wear sunglasses all day,
Claiming they're part of the ballet.
While octopuses knit, so sublime,
Creating tales in vibrant rhyme.

Deep Calling to Deep

Giant squids with juggling skills,
Making waves with oceanic thrills.
"Do you want fries with that?" they cheer,
As jellyfish giggle, flinging their beer.

A whale sings, "Can you hear me now?"
Echoes bounce off each yellow cow.
Cheeky dolphins, they leap and twist,
Creating splashes you can't resist.

Songs of the Wind-Swept Waters

A crab's got rhythm, he taps his claw,
To the sailor's songs, he gives a paw.
While gulls compete in a grumpy debate,
Who's the best bird? Oh, they can't wait!

Mermaids whisper secrets with flair,
While pirates search for lost underwear.
Octopus bands jamming till dusk,
With sea cucumbers, they're all a-bust!

Echoing the Call of Yore

Bubbles rise like ancient tales,
Dancing fish wear tiny veils,
Seashells giggle in the tide,
As crabs play tag and sidle wide.

Old ships whisper in the wind,
With tales of pirates and their kin,
The gulls cry out a silly song,
As dolphins dive and twirl along.

Currents of Celestial Remembrance

Starfish stargaze on the shore,
Pretending they're the famous four,
Seahorses prance like they're in style,
While octopuses juggle all the while.

The tides tell jokes in a salty tone,
About a clam that wanted a throne,
A shrimp that danced with a floating leaf,
While the seaweed giggled in disbelief.

Beneath the Weaving Waters

Mermaids knitting nets of laughter,
Their yarns spun tales, happily ever after,
Crabs in tuxedos plotting a show,
As sea cucumbers steal the glow.

A whale hums tunes from long ago,
While fish do the cha-cha in a row,
Turtles waddle to a groovy beat,
Each wave a grand encore, oh so sweet!

Ancestral Echoes of the Deep

Fishes whisper secrets in the brine,
Of an ancient company of sardines fine,
While starfish lounge in their coral beds,
Spinning yarns of lost pirate threads.

Jellyfish float with jelly-filled dreams,
As laughter bubbles up in beams,
Anemones sway, throwing a ball,
In the grandest underwater hall!

Driftwood Diaries

On a log I found a text,
Written by a fish or vexed,
It said, 'Beware of playful tides,
They tickle toes and take your rides.'

Seagulls laugh in raucous glee,
They steal my fries while I sip tea,
The ocean's got a funny bone,
Waves giggle at my sunburned own.

An Odyssey in Saltwater

With flip-flops on, I brave the foam,
A crab yells, 'Hey! This is my home!'
I dance while dodging jellyfish,
Who seem to have their own wild wish.

A whale nearby sings off-key,
Makes dolphins snicker, 'Can you hear me?'
Ocean floors could host a choir,
Their concert's one I'd soon retire!

Memories of Mermaid Melodies

Mermaids hum their tunes so light,
But trip on shells on moonlit nights,
They laugh and splash, it's quite the scene,
As fish throw pearls, a playful sheen.

With seaweed wigs and fishy flair,
They call for sailors unaware,
Who lose their ships to giggles sweet,
And end up dancing with their feet!

The Depths Remember

In deepest water, laughter flows,
A giant squid with ticklish toes,
He tells of dreams beneath the waves,
Where every sea creature misbehaves.

Octopuses juggle with great glee,
While turtles race, oh what a spree!
Their underwater shenanigans,
Are laughter echoes, upside-down spins.

Nautical Whispers Across Ages

In a ship made of dreams, fish sing in style,
Old crabs wear top hats, strutting a mile.
Seagulls gossip 'bout the tide's crazy dance,
While octopuses twirl in a humorous trance.

Mermaids play chess with a wise old squid,
Whispering secrets that time never hid.
Starfish cheerlead on the rocks up above,
As jellyfish float on a wave full of love.

Where Ocean Meets Memory

Waves chuckle softly, a ticklish delight,
Shells gossip about fish in the moonlight.
Turtles recall when they raced with the sun,
While dolphins joke, 'Hey! We've just begun!'

Sandcastles rise, then giggle and fall,
As crabs play soccer, a rousing ball.
In tidal laughter, the past finds its tune,
With treasures that shimmer beneath the full moon.

A Tidal Touch of Time

Frothy waves wave to the gulls in the air,
Clams tell tall tales, if you stop to stare.
A fish in a bowtie forgets where it swam,
While turtles recite poems, oh, what a jam!

Saltwater giggles light up the blue,
As seaweed sways to an ancient review.
The humor of finned friends travels so far,
Each splash is a memory, a quirky memoir.

Rippled Reverberations of Yesteryears

A floaty octopus knits under the sun,
While barnacles chuckle, 'Oh, isn't this fun?'
The waves spin yarns from the years gone by,
As snappy sea urchins join in with a sigh.

Kelp forests sway in a rhythm of glee,
As fish tell tall tales of a lost bumblebee.
With laughter and bubbles, the ocean does cheer,
For every wave echoes a giggle from here.

Odes to the Ocean's Legacy

In a salty embrace with a jellyfish whack,
The octopus giggles from its seaweed stack.
Seashells gossip, they've got tales galore,
Of crabs having tantrums and fish that snore.

The dolphins do flips, while the turtles just chill,
While starfish conspire to give humans a thrill.
Seahorses strut in their tiny parade,
While clams keep on clamoring, 'We've got it made!'.

Echoing Waves of History

Oh, the waves tell a story, but shhh, don't you dare,
The mermaids are whispering secrets to air.
They've seen ships sink, and they've watched sailors pitch,

While a crab in a top hat plans to find the rich.

The barnacles sing, in their crusty old choir,
Of pirate gold hidden just o'er a wire.
Fish wear sunglasses, as they chill on the reef,
While dolphins laugh loud, at the catfish's grief.

The Forgotten Atlas

An ancient map rests at the deep ocean floor,
While fish play charades, and wonder what's more.
The sea cucumbers plotting world domination,
But all they can do is sway with temptation.

With bubbles of laughter, the kraken does dance,
Daring old ships for a funny romance.
While turtles argue over the best speed,
It seems that the ocean's their favorite steed.

Whims of the Water's Depths

A whale sings a tune, but it sounds like a joke,
While squids juggle pearls and the seaweed just chokes.
The sunken ships whisper of treasures untold,
As sailors play poker with sharks feeling bold.

Starfish do yoga, aligning their rays,
While clownfish chuckle in their silly ways.
With currents a-twirl, the ocean has flair,
As it's chuckling along, with a watery care.

Whispers of Forgotten Waves

Bubbles giggle, secrets shared,
Fish wear hats, they're quite prepared.
Crabs play cards on the sandy deck,
While seagulls squawk, what the heck!

Starfish gossip, stars they're not,
Jellyfish dance, an elegant knot.
Octopuses juggle their lunch with flair,
A clam once claimed it could fly in air!

Seashells whisper tales of yore,
Of pirate maps and treasure galore.
But mostly they just talk of tides,
And how the seaweed sometimes hides.

Each wave a laugh, each splash a grin,
Throwing us memories, deep within.
Who knew the ocean had such a flair?
With all this humor, who needs fresh air?

Echoes of Time Beneath the Tide

Barnacles cling with a stubborn cheer,
Turtles debate who's the fastest here.
Anemones wave like hands in the crowd,
While dolphins flip, and they're laughably loud!

Clownfish joke, hiding in their base,
"Why did the crab never leave his place?"
Why? Because to the end, he'd always stick,
And with those pincers, he's quite the pick!

Coral castles, full of jest,
Invite octopi and shrimp for a fest.
They tell tall tales of sunken ships,
With treasure chests that hold no chips.

Echoes of laughter fill the brine,
Whispering secrets, not one of mine.
In the depths of the blue, all tales unwind,
Each ripple a chuckle, a tale well-timed!

Legends Carved in Coral

Once a hammerhead forgot his tool,
Swam round and round in an epic duel.
Clownfish laughed till they nearly cried,
"Did you know? Your brain's where you hide!"

Oysters push pearls just for the thrill,
"What's your secret?" "Just stay still!"
They whisper jokes to the passing shells,
In the underwater world, laughter dwells.

Starry skies above, starlit below,
The creatures share fables, letting them flow.
And deep in the dark, don't be surprised,
A sleepy squid yawns, and it's widely recognized!

The coral giggles in a colorful way,
As sea turtles glide, in a humorous sway.
In this realm of mirth, the old tales soar,
From legends carved on the ocean's floor!

The Dancer of the Deep

Ballroom fish twirl in a grand display,
Where polka dots sway in the bluesy play.
A shrimp in a tux leads a merry parade,
While a flounder trips, but isn't dismayed.

Tangled in seaweed, a crab takes a chance,
Declaring his right to join in the dance.
With every flip the turtles create,
The sea becomes a party, oh how great!

The mermaids chuckle, flipping their hair,
As sea creatures whirl in a waltz so rare.
"Did you hear the one about the fish with no hook?"
"Don't worry, his story's a real page-turner book!"

In the depths of the stage, hilarity reigns,
As jellyfish jiggle, letting go of their chains.
So join in the fun, let the currents take sway,
For in this big blue, absurdity soon leads the way!

Beneath the Horizon's Gaze

Beneath the sky, where seagulls tease,
Waves bring tales of sandcastles with ease.
A fish once told a tall, fishy tale,
Of the time he almost joined the mail!

Crabs have their meetings, all secret and sly,
Discussing the best way to wave goodbye.
Starfish form stars, but they lack direction,
Their thoughts float away in pure reflection.

The dolphins giggle, in watery dance,
They flip and they splash, just taking a chance.
"Why don't we surf?" one slyly suggests,
But seaweed's the one who always protests!

So if you listen, when skies turn to grey,
You might hear the ocean's most wacky play.
From mermaid's jokes to octopus pranks,
The shoreline's a stage for funny hijinks!

The Coral's Chronicle

In reefs so lively, where colors collide,
Corals gossip, in their colorful pride.
One claims to remember the day it was young,
When it danced with a whale, to a seaweed sung!

Anemones chuckle, their tentacles sway,
"Who needs a date when you can catch rays?"
They tease the clownfish in bright, silly hats,
"Come on, join us, leave those boring old chats!"

Octopus artists, with eight limbs to twirl,
Paint scenes of fish in a watery swirl.
A tiny shrimp insists, with a flick of its tail,
"Guys, let's make a mural of the great ocean trail!"

As bubbles of laughter rise to the top,
The corals keep secrets, but never will stop.
They giggle and wiggle, like a party gone wild,
In a kingdom of laughter, where everyone's styled!

Secrets Held in Shells

Ears pressed to shells, secrets echo true,
A clam says the waves have a grand ball to do.
"They'll serve sea cucumbers and wiggly eels,
And prizes for fish with the best dance feels!"

Turtles in shades share gossip they hear,
"Did you see the whale? Oh, it's lost, my dear!"
They chuckle together, "Throw it a map,
Or at least a big shell for a fancy wrap!"

The hermit crabs shuffle, don't mind losing homes,
As they argue whose shell has the shiniest chrome.
One pulls his frazzled self out with a grin,
"Let's make it a game, who's the true shell king?"

So wander the beaches, let the whispers flow,
For the whispers of shells hold more than you know.
From the drama of fish to the tales of the tides,
Each shell's a reminder of where humor hides!

The Great Blue Tapestry

Spun like a quilt, the ocean's wide tales,
Where each wave's a stitch, and laughter prevails.
The anglerfish lights up, in a comical beam,
While sea lions juggle, like a circus dream!

Schools of fish swirl, in synchronized glee,
They practice their moves like an underwater spree.
"Cannonball time!" one boldly exclaims,
As they leap from the reef, playing silly games!

A grouper declares, "Let's have a grand feast,
With plankton and zooplankton, to say the least!"
But the squids hold their ink, and giggle in thrill,
"At least save some snacks for our underwater grill!"

So all across currents, where laughter rings clear,
The ocean spins stories that tickle the ear.
From reefs to the abyss, they weave bright displays,
In the great blue tapestry, humor always stays!

Remnants of Lost Mariners

A sailor lost his favorite hat,
Drifting with the waves and splat!
He swears it's still out there, quite bold,
Chatting with fish, or so I'm told.

A message in a bottle, he sent,
But it drifted off, not quite well-meant.
It landed in a crab's feast instead,
Gone are the words he bravely said.

One parrot found a treasure map,
But all it led to was a nap!
He dreams of riches, golds so fine,
Meanwhile, he's snacking on old brine.

So if you swim and hear some laughter,
It's just the ghosts of sailors after.
They've lost their way, but not their cheer,
Making merry, year after year!

Lullabies of the Abyss

In the deep where the seaweed sways,
Mermaids sing in oddball ways.
With fishy tunes and rhymes so silly,
They dance and giggle, oh so frilly.

An octopus plays the ukulele,
Fooling whales with tunes quite snaily.
The turtles clap with flippers wide,
While the squid serves snacks with pride.

Crabs form a band with pots and cans,
Trying to sway all the ocean's fans.
But their rhythm's off and feet too quick,
They tumble and roll, oh what a trick!

So down below, where shadows creep,
Turn down the lights, and count some sheep.
The lullabies are pure delight,
Sailing with laughter through the night!

Shadows of Sunken Ships

Ghost ships sail with a creaky wail,
Their captains lost, they tell a tale.
Of treasure hunts that went awry,
Chasing squids who wave goodbye!

They surf on waves of tangled sea grass,
Throwing parties, oh what a sass!
With merfolk jesters causing a stir,
Hiding loot inside a fur.

An old sailor once searched for rum,
Instead found a clam that went 'thum!'
It clanked and clattered, causing a fuss,
"Now that's treasure! Let's ride the bus!"

So if you spot a hull or two,
With shadows dancing, don't misconstrue!
They're throwing a bash, with jellyfish lights,
Living it up on those watery nights!

The Ocean's Silent Witness

Waves whisper secrets to the shore,
'You won't believe what happened before!'
The jellyfish giggle at the sight,
Of sailors trying to take flight.

A dolphin dives with a flip and a spin,
While a crab just sits, wearing a grin.
Each splash a story, a giggle, a glee,
Fish are in stitches, just you wait and see!

A whale sings low, sounds like a troll,
Echoing tales of their underwater stroll.
Meanwhile, sea turtles roll on their backs,
In a shell-shaped Volvo, plotting their tracks!

So listen close while you sip your tea,
For the ocean's laughter is wild and free.
With every wave that breaks on the sand,
It's a giggly gossip from a watery land!

Chronicles Encased in Coral

Little fish in a bustling school,
Swapping tales, oh what a jewel!
A crab recounts his clawing fights,
While all the clams roll with delight.

An octopus, in a sneaky guise,
Mocks the sharks with playful lies.
Seashells giggle, waves applaud,
As laughter spreads like a proud facade.

Jellyfish dance with otherworldly grace,
While seaweed twirls in a snazzy race.
Old barnacles with wisdom stare,
Secret jokes of salty air.

In this oceanic comedy troupe,
Every bubble forms a scoop.
They sketch the tales in sandy scrolls,
Mirth and mischief, the ocean's goals.

Echoes of the Briny Deep

Echoes bounce off the ocean floor,
As fishy gossip settles the score.
A whale's laugh is a booming charm,
While squids giggle, causing alarm.

The turtles slow for a cheeky chat,
With crabs adorned in hats quite fat.
Anemones sharing salty puns,
Punchlines drifted with the morning runs.

Starfish exchange their mili-tales,
About shipwrecks and pirate fails.
With each laugh, the current sways,
Bubbling joy for endless days.

A salty breeze carries the jest,
As wave-dancers twirl, all impressed.
Underneath, the sandworms wriggle,
In this salty sea, laughter's the giggle.

Olfactory Memories of the Ocean

With every splash, a scent does rise,
Of kelp and salt, oh what a surprise!
Anchovies prank with fishy bliss,
While seabirds circle, not to miss.

Sardines sing of a taco night,
While mackerels flaunt their sprightly bites.
From beach to deep, aromas merge,
Zesty tales in the currents surge.

A sea cucumber takes center stage,
With funky odors, all the rage.
While dolphins twist, bubble, and cheer,
Sniffing delights, the catch of the year.

The barnacles hum a tilted tune,
In scents of fish and sweet maroon.
As waves roll in with fragrant glee,
The ocean's laughter, oh so free.

Musings of the Moonlit Deep

Under the moon, reflections play,
Fishy dreams drift on display.
A plankton poet scribbles in light,
While critters laugh at their salty plight.

Clownfish wonder, "Are we that funny?"
As they wiggle by, eyes sparkling sunny.
A sleepy dolphin lets out a snore,
Startling a grouper next door!

Puffers puff up in a fit of mirth,
While sea urchins boast of their prickly worth.
Cranky conchs, with their wise old show,
Know every punchline the ocean will throw.

With every ripple that whispers near,
Comedic tales echo throughout here.
In this watery world, laughter's the key,
A joyful secret, shared by the sea.

Secrets of the Ocean's Heart

Beneath the waves, fish tell their jokes,
Seahorses dance, and starfish poke.
Octopuses juggle with eight funny arms,
Whales hum tunes with their aquatic charms.

Crabs in tuxedos stroll along the sand,
Chatting with clams, both wary and grand.
"Have you heard of the shipwreck's grand feast?
It's rumored they'll serve a most curious beast."

The jellyfish float, all giddy and bright,
Trading old stories, by the moon's soft light.
"Why don't fish play piano? It's hard to fin!
They've no fingers at all, just scales on their skin!"

With bubbles of laughter, the deep sea thrives,
Each creature a storyteller, full of lives.
In this secret world, where the happy hearts play,
The ocean holds secrets that tickle and sway.

Tides of Forgotten Tales

Once a crab dreamed of being a king,
With a crown made of shells, what a funny thing!
He declared himself ruler of all sandy shores,
While fish rolled their eyes and swam in scores.

A wise old turtle with stories to share,
Told tales of the ships lost in salty despair.
But the gulls just squawked, "It's all just a hoot!
Better watch out for that seagull in a suit!"

The tide pulls the moon, like it's in on a joke,
As dolphins join in, and the surf starts to poke.
"Did you hear about the crab who ran for the shore?
He missed the catch, but found a new chore!"

In this vibrant splash of laughter and cheer,
The ocean's past holds no need for fear.
With each wave that crashes, a giggle goes by,
As the tides of forgotten tales float in the sky.

Beneath the Blue Expanse

In the blue expanse, a clownfish grins wide,
Telling his puns with a flamboyant pride.
"Why did the coral go out for a run?
To catch the attention of the bright setting sun!"

Giant squids chuckle, with ink on their face,
As they mimic the humans, so clumsy in grace.
"Why don't pirates play cards in the deep?
They're afraid of the sharks—no promises they'll keep!"

Anemones sway, with a giggle or two,
Their laughter a dance in the aquatic blue.
"I saw a mermaid with three left feet,
She slipped on a wave—now that's no small feat!"

In this realm of chuckles, where sea life cavorts,
Every critter knows how to share funny reports.
Beneath the water, where silliness reigns,
The laughter of currents flows through their veins.

Legends Carried by Currents

Legends are woven in bubbles and foam,
Tales of a turtle who never found home.
He swam round and round, with a wink and a snort,
Claiming he'd found a treasure report!

Fish gather 'round as he draws in the sand,
"I've seen a great beast, with a cold, floppy hand!"
The crowd gasps and giggles, they lean in to see,
As the turtle keeps spinning this tale with glee.

A clam chimes in, with a glimmering sound,
"Did you hear about the lobster who lost a leg round?
He started a band, and the crabs joined him too,
Playing rock in the reef, what a sight to pursue!"

As currents caress and waves splash with flair,
The legends unveil with a giggle to share.
In salty embrace, tales float and they swirl,
Where every sea creature is part of the whirl.

Resonance of Riveting Waves

A crab wore shades, looking fly,
With jellyfish jumping in the sky.
They sang a tune, quite offbeat,
As seashells danced with groovy feet.

A dolphin tried to breakdance,
But slipped on seaweed, lost his chance.
A starfish laughed, rolled with glee,
Saying, 'Some talent you don't see!'

An octopus flipped pancakes at dawn,
While clams kept clamoring on and on.
They created a café by the pier,
Where drinks are served with a splash of cheer.

The waves must giggle, splash, and crash,
Underneath the foam, they make quite a splash.
With every tide, a chuckle flows,
In the salty breeze, the humor grows.

Tales of the Moonlit Waters

The moon took a dip, but forgot her clothes,
While fish threw a party, striking poses.
They danced to the rhythm of the night's cool breeze,
Making waves of laughter, calling friends with ease.

A gull swooped down, claiming the stage,
With a stand-up act, all the fish engaged.
A whale cracked jokes, quite grand and tall,
While seaweed giggled, right by the coral wall.

'Why do the boats never seem to find?
It's all in the tide, they're too far behind!'
Echoes of joy in a watery night,
The creatures unleashed their playful delight.

As the stars twinkled and fish gently swayed,
A clam brought cupcakes, beautifully displayed.
With icing of foam and sprinkles from sand,
Those moonlit waters had laughter well planned.

The Silent Lament of the Ocean

An octopus sighed, all tentacles drooped,
'Why must my friends all be thoughtless or stooped?'
He missed the old days, when sharks were the kings,
Now they swim past, ignoring his flings.

A whale moped around, feeling quite low,
'All this deep water makes me feel slow.'
But then a dolphin spun, what a show!
And suddenly everyone felt the glow.

They threw a parade, with seaweed confetti,
While clams tapped their shells, oh so ready.
'Let's lighten up, drop the blues of the sea,'
The ocean agreed, 'Let's just let it be!'

Now the ocean hums a whimsical tune,
With schools of fish dancing beneath the moon.
And though it laments in the soft, salty sway,
Even waves can laugh at the end of the day.

Forgotten Shores of Antiquity

On shores long lost, where sea dogs still bark,
A treasure map led straight to the park.
Where crabs seek gold with pirate flair,
They dig for trinkets, but find old hair!

An ancient turtle with tales to tell,
Said, 'In my day, we danced quite well.'
But the seagulls just snickered and flew away,
While the surf chimed in with a playful sway.

Every broken bottle held a wish, it's true,
A fortune cookie from the ocean's view.
But instead of wisdom, they just got jokes,
With fishy punchlines and laughter from folks.

So gather the shells, raise a toast to the tide,
For history's humor, we don't need to hide.
With each crashing wave, don't let the past bore,
The forgotten shores still hold laughter galore!

Traces of Time on the Tide

Sandcastles rise, then fall away,
As waves don't care for things we say.
A crab in a hat, with quite the flair,
Dancing to rhythms found in the air.

Seashells whisper tales of old,
Of pirate treasures and seas of gold.
But when I listen, I hear no loot,
Just stinky fish and a lost old boot.

Jellyfish bob like they own the place,
Giving tired waves a quirky face.
They drift and swirl with a jelly-like glee,
Not a care in the world, just fancy and free.

So if you find a crusty report,
Of mermaid mischief and fishy court,
Know that beneath the waves' playful chime,
Lies a laughter-filled, wavy old rhyme.

Constellations Beneath the Surface

Starfish lounge where lights go dim,
Counting its friends on a whim.
An octopus plays hide and seek,
While sea cucumbers look rather meek.

Somersaulting dolphins in a line,
Creating artworks, oh so divine.
The gulls look down with a judgmental stare,
As if to say, 'What's happening there?'

Coral reefs giggle, oh what a sight,
With fishes prancing in sheer delight.
But don't take a selfie, they might pout,
Fish fame is fickle, no room for doubt.

In waters vast, the punchlines climb,
Giggling through rhythms of splashing rhyme.
Don't forget your snorkel and fun-loving grin,
For beneath this blue is where laughs begin.

Shimmering Stories of the Past

Bubbles float up carrying tales,
Of shipwrecks, pirates, and slimy snails.
A fish with glasses reads the news,
While the seahorses share some old blues.

Lobsters in tuxedos take to the floor,
Waltzing through currents, they always want more.
An eel cracks jokes with a toothy grin,
While clams just sit looking all prim.

Oh, what a ball, the kraken's shy,
Twirling with jelly, oh my, oh my!
They all have quirks, and they all have flair,
Even the barnacles combing their hair.

So grab your floaties, bring all your cheer,
For the deep-sea chuckles are ringing near.
Flip the waves, dive deep in the fun,
Nature's a circus, let's all be one!

The Depths We Never Knew

Down where the guppies get their groove,
And fish with mustaches start to move.
A turtle in shades claims it all,
While squids argue who's king of the hall.

Beneath the surface, secrets float,
On water's sigh, the legends wrote.
Cracks in the coral hold stories anew,
Of bucket-listers who never quite grew.

Schools of fish gossip in blinks,
As dolphins send knitted thoughts in links.
They laugh at the anchors, rusty and old,
In this underwater world of mischief bold.

So cast out your worries, let the waves guide,
Find joy in the bubbles, in laughter abide.
The depths are a playground, bright and absurd,
Where every splash is a giggle unheard.

Phantoms in the Foam

In bubbles where the fish do dance,
Ghostly whispers take their chance.
Octopuses wear hats with flair,
While crabs tap out a tune with care.

Seagulls join the seaside band,
Dropping beats like guacamole stand.
A sea turtle swings by to groove,
In shell-tacular moves, they smoothly prove.

Mermaids trade their tails for shoes,
And sing about their pickle blues.
With jellyfish lights to guide the way,
They're raving under waves all day!

So, if you hear a splash and cheer,
Don't fret; it's just the ocean's leer.
For in the foam where ghosts may beam,
They know how to have fun, it seems!

The Underwater Library

Beneath the waves, a library floats,
With books that smell like salty oats.
Fish read tales of pirate glee,
While dolphins flip through history.

A crab is chief of circulation,
With a pinch, he runs the operation.
Seaweed stacks lean to and fro,
As mermaids whisper, 'Shh, not so loud, you know!'

The librarian shark swims by with grace,
Giving each fish a knowing face.
'Read this one—it's bound to provoke,'
As an octopus makes a joke and croaks.

In this sunken site, all is grand,
With stories spun from sand to sand.
So grab a book, don't feel shy,
Here the waves laugh as they pass by!

Flotsam of Time

Drifting objects on the tide,
A rubber duck with nowhere to hide.
Ancient spoons and bottles bright,
Becoming stars in the ocean's light.

A pirate's hat floats past my face,
While sea-otters claim it with grace.
They make it a throne, oh it's quite sublime,
Laughing and chill, lost in time.

Old flip-flops start a dance-off spree,
With seagrass partners and a jellyfish DJ.
The beachcombers join in with a cheer,
As the ocean laughs, 'Time's nothing to fear!'

So grab some flotsam, let's keep the beat,
With treasures that bring laughter so sweet.
In this watery world, the fun won't quit,
For every lost thing has a story to fit!

Depths of Distant Shores

Down in the depths where the sun don't peek,
A turtle's telling tales so unique.
With glow-in-the-dark fish as his crew,
They navigate where the currents flow too.

A whale with a tux laughs loud and bright,
Spinning the yarns of starry night.
'Did you hear about the crab in Paris?'
He dined on snails, oh how outrageous!

The anemones dance with quirky grace,
While sea horses compete in a wacky race.
They wear tiny hats and sprint with flair,
As playful bubbles fill the salty air.

So if you drop below the foam,
Join the laughter in their ocean home.
For in those depths, the humor's alive,
And every creature knows how to thrive!

Fragments of the Abyssal Past

Once a fish wore a suit and tie,
He swam past a crab who asked him why.
"I'm off to a meeting, don't let me be late!"
The crab just chuckled, "Well, isn't that great!"

A dolphin jumped up with a splash so bold,
"I found a treasure that glittered like gold!"
But it turned out to be just old fishy scales,
Now they're making jokes of those epic fail tales.

A clam threw a party with bubbly sea foam,
While barnacles tapped to their own little tome.
The jellyfish glowed as they danced in delight,
But the octopus slipped, what a hilarious sight!

So here in the depths, laughter fills the blue,
With fishy tomfoolery, always something new!
Our ocean is crazy, with tales that are vast,
A place where the silly is forever cast.

Whispers Beneath the Waves

A turtle once whispered, "I'm quite the slowpoke!"
The fish gathered 'round, all in on the joke.
"With every shell I carry, I'm quite built to last!"
They laughed till they cried, what a splash in the past!

An eel with a quirk liked to tie himself knots,
He swam through the reef, showing off what he's got.
The clownfish all gasped and began to applaud,
But the eel then got tangled and that made them all nod!

A starfish flipped burgers on a grill made of sand,
While seaweed declared it a culinary brand!
The krill hoped for seconds, they giggled and pranced,
As the whole ocean's crowd joined in the dance.

So down in the depths, the fun never ends,
With whispers and laughter from sea critter friends!
A world full of chuckles, where each wave does sway,
With giggles and grins wrapped in salty bouquet!

Echoes of Salt and Time

A seagull named Fred wore a sailor's hat,
He thought he was clever, the cleverest brat.
He squawked all day long about treasure to find,
But it turned out to be just a sandwich left behind!

In the depths, the sea cucumber waved hello,
"I'm more than a veggie, I dance in the flow!"
The shrimp did a jig, with each tiny clop,
Said the cucumber, "Hey, stop! I can't dance, I just flop!"

The narwhal got stuck trying to slide 'round a rock,
"I'm a unicorn, see?" he said with a shock!
But the others just laughed, they were rolling with glee,
"You're part whale, part fish, not a horse, can't you see?"

So echoes resound through the blue and the foam,
Where creatures of laughter and bubbly hearts roam!
In this playful world, no one can keep straight,
Life's a cheerful mess, isn't it great?

Chronicles of the Deep

A fish with a mustache wore glasses of gold,
He started a school for the young and the bold.
"First lesson: Always be quick on your fins!"
But the lobster just laughed, "Do we learn any sins?"

The octopus bobbed, trying to spin round and round,
But he spun too fast, and fell flat on the ground.
With a flourish, he said, "I just meant to show!"
But the blowfish just snortled, "Yeah, we all saw the show!"

The pufferfish blew up with a joke to be told,
"I'm inflatable now, but I'm just as bold!"
While others just giggled, not taking him serious,
He puffed up again, becoming delirious!

So in this strange place where the currents mix,
Life is a comedy of scales and of tricks!
With every great tale floating 'round in the blue,
The chronicles here are bizarre but true!

Ripples of Remembrance

In a splashy old world, fish wear glasses,
They think they are wise, but just swim in masses.
Crabs tell tall tales of clams with a hat,
While octopuses giggle at the seahorse chat.

Seagulls drop wisdom like crumbs in a feast,
While dolphins do math like a curious beast.
A starfish claims he once walked on the land,
But flip-flop shoes won't be part of his brand.

Turtles play chess with the waves to their side,
Jellyfish playing jump rope, what a wild ride!
The coral stands silent, an observer of fun,
While the seaweed dances, "Oh, we're not done!"

So gather 'round, friends, and lend me an ear,
The ocean keeps secrets, oh my, let's all cheer!
With giggles and bubbles, we'll weave the old tales,
In laughter and joy, we'll set our own sails.

Waters Whispering Histories

The waves tell stories with a splishy-splash,
Of mermaid ballet and a kraken's big crash.
A sardine school whispers, "Not much to see!"
As clowns of the ocean, we swim wild and free.

Gulls swoop to gossip, spilling tea on the brine,
"Did you hear about Norman? He thought he was fine!
He tried to impress with a dance on a wave,
But slipped on a clam - sweet Norman, so brave!"

The seafoam chuckles, a frothy old chap,
With tales of the sailors who fell for a nap.
The barnacles laugh as they cling to the rocks,
Reminding the fish of their mismatched socks.

And when the tide grins with a bubbly wave,
The flounders break dance like they're trying to rave.
Each splash echoes laughter, what a joyous spree,
For the water's wise whispers bring sepia glee!

Legends in the Depths

In the depths, there's Danny, a fish with a flip,
Who tells tales of treasure and sea monster trips.
While sharks roll their eyes, never caught in a bind,
But they giggle at eels who in knots are confined.

There's a sponge with a ukulele, singing so bright,
To crabs in a circle, dancing deep in the night.
The mackerel watch, slightly envious too,
"Can we join in a jig? Oh dear, what a view!"

A ray spins around, gets dizzy with pride,
While clams gossip hard, but they've nothing to hide.
Old turtles swap yarns, their stories so long,
In the blue, floated laughter can seldom be wrong.

So dive deep, my friends, into chuckles and lore,
With each wave we ride, we'll find so much more.
The ocean's a stage where the salt meets the sweet,
With legends that tickle our fins and our feet!

The Submerged Saga

In a cove full of laughter, the fish do a meet,
With anemones popping like popcorn to eat.
Under rocks, they conjure, with bubbles and cheer,
"Did you hear of the shrimp who lost all of his gear?"

Pufferfish stand up, with puffs of delight,
While turtles roll over – oh what a sight!
Seashells trade secrets, a wink and a glance,
Those pearls in our hearts love to shimmy and dance.

With currents of giggles as bright as the sun,
The narwhals all gather, for jokes that are fun.
They swim through the tales that the barnacles sing,
In this underwater world, laughter's the king!

So let's raise the anchor, cast worries away,
With each flick of a fin, come join in the play!
In the depths of the ocean, joy never fades,
For the submerged saga will always cascade!

Songs of Swells and Stills

When waves feel like a giant's sneeze,
They tickle boats with playful tease.
Fish dance like they're at a ball,
While seagulls squawk and have a brawl.

A dolphin jokes with a splashy flip,
He claims he's never lost a trip.
Jellyfish float like blobs of goo,
Waving goodbye as they bid adieu.

Salted air gives the wind a grin,
As crabs play poker under their skin.
Seashells whisper secrets of old,
About pirates' gold that was never sold.

With every tide, a tale will swell,
Of mermaids who sing and ring a bell.
The ocean's laughter echoes wide,
As it tickles every silly side.

Nautical Nostalgia

A sailor's hat, three sizes too big,
Tangled in knots, oh what a jig!
Old sea stories that make you grin,
Like that time the fish got under his skin.

The compass spins with dizzy flair,
While barnacles play truth or dare.
An octopus dressed in style so neat,
Will challenge anyone to a dance-off feat.

Old boots are floating, lost in a game,
While jellybeans try to stake their claim.
Whale songs ring like a goofy tune,
As they serenade the cuddly raccoon.

Every wave tells tales of jest,
With seagulls critiquing the sailor's best.
A ship sails on, full of glee,
Navigating through this funny spree!

The Abyssal Archive

Bottles float, all filled with dreams,
As the ocean giggles and slyly schemes.
A treasure chest, with socks and beans,
Where every lost item truly preens.

Anemones dance like pom-pom girls,
While starfish spin in their glittery swirls.
The depths hold secrets, both odd and bright,
Like fish in top hats, what a sight!

Old shipwrecks whisper tales so absurd,
Of rum-soaked parrot and a fish that preferred,
To ride on waves like a lazy cat,
With a snort and a chuckle, "How about that?"

In the watery void, there's laughter to be found,
As echoes of joy play round and round.
For every deep, mysterious lore,
There's a silly joke we can't ignore.

Mysterious Mariner's Map

A map with squiggles, like a doodle spree,
Leads to chocolates and a quirky tree.
Mystery bubbles like a cork popped right,
Where X marks the spot for a mud pie fight.

Tangled directions send sailors astray,
While sea cows giggle, "Not this way!"
Clams laugh so hard, they turn purple blue,
As the map shows a route to a grand old zoo.

With a compass that's lost its mind in the sun,
A pirate's quest just turned into fun.
Sailing through clouds of blueberry fluff,
Chasing adventures that never get tough.

So grab your maps, don't take a nap,
Join the silly crew for a laughter trap.
With every twist, and every cheer,
The ocean calls, "Come join us here!"

Timeless Treasures Beneath Waves

In depths where treasures fiercely lie,
A sock from Neptune floats on by.
A goldfish dreams of being a king,
While barnacles dance and seashells sing.

Old rusted anchors laugh and tease,
They've seen more than you'd believe, if you please.
A pirate's parrot scoffs at the fate,
As clams share gossip about a mate.

A mermaid with a glittering tail,
Collects old spoons and a broken nail.
"What's next?" she asks, diving deeper still,
"I've lost my schedule and my thrill!"

The currents whisper jokes of the past,
As fish parade in a splashing blast.
Who knew the ocean could be so grand?
With treasures trading tales, hand in hand.

Financial Folklore of Fathoms

Down in the depths where the dollars gleam,
Octopuses trade with a glittering dream.
Starfish invest in seaweed stocks,
While crustaceans plot investment blocks.

The fish have stocks that gleam and sway,
And crabs are counting shells all day.
"Divers are in, investors too!"
But pearls don't pay, they just look new!

Squids hold meetings with serious faces,
Discussing market dips in hidden places.
Mussels hold fortunes under the tide,
Forgetting their growth as they open wide.

A dolphin declares, "I've called it right!"
"Invest in sea cucumbers, a good sight!"
Above, the humans work with greed,
While below, the ocean takes its lead.

Tides of Forgotten Lore

The tides bring tales from the days of yore,
Of shipwrecks that snore on the ocean floor.
A clam with a secret, a fish with a grin,
They whisper of treasures lost in the din.

Old wavy maps tell stories of glee,
Of sailors who danced with a raucous spree.
A seagull's squawk shares a joke or two,
While the jellyfish giggles, "What's new with you?"

At night, the waves glow with laughter and mirth,
As starfish retell their unforgettable birth.
"Remember that time we all got trapped?
That crab was so mad, it nearly snapped!"

And as the moon watches, full of delight,
The ocean keeps secrets, hidden from sight.
Each splash, a chuckle, each ripple, a jest,
In the depths of the deep, where laughter is best.

Waves Carry the Stories

Waves roll in with tales to share,
Of goofy fish and tales beyond compare.
A dolphin's giggle, a sea turtle's wink,
These tales percolate faster than you think.

Crabs do the cha-cha, snails take a ride,
Whales weave ballads like flowing tide.
"Listen closely," calls a starry star,
"Every glimmer is a story from afar."

Seashells conspire, passing whispers near,
About a whale who swam with no fear.
A porous sponge tells of soggy sprints,
And the octopus grins, "Oh, where's my prints?"

With every splash, a laugh erupts,
As the ocean's humor easily corrupts.
So take a dip and dive down low,
You'll hear the waves, where the fun tides flow!

The Blue World's Memory Lane

In the blue depths, fish kick back,
Telling tales of their wild snack attack.
A jellyfish floats, with no care,
Wobbling like it's lost in the air.

Crabs hold court in their sandy throne,
Arguing over a forgotten bone.
Starfish laugh at the barnacle's plight,
Claiming they're royalty, holding on tight.

Seashells gossip on a sunny beach,
Moaning about all the things they can't teach.
Octopuses juggle to earn applause,
But ink spills out, causing loud guffaws.

A whale swims by, with wisdom so grand,
Spouting water, creating a band.
Fish breakdance in a swirling display,
Throwing a party, come join the fray!

Reflections on Deeds Beneath the Foam

Turtles gossip on a driftwood plank,
Discussing the state of the ocean bank.
One says, 'I saw a dolphin eat foam!'
The others laugh, 'No way, that's not home!'

Crabs have meetings with a secret stash,
Debating the merits of a lucky splash.
Mermaids trade wigs made from seaweed strands,
Chasing sea turtles, who make silly plans.

Fish in a school, always in sync,
Got caught playing hide and seek with a wink.
Pufferfish puffed, trying to be sly,
Then snickered as big sharks swam on by.

Bubbles rise high, filled with giggles and cheer,
A clam sings loudly, but no one can hear.
In the ocean's depths, jesters reside,
With fishy punchlines, they'll always abide!

Ancient Whales' Lament

An old whale sighs, his tales are a riot,
Once he swam with a ship, maybe he'll try it.
His friends, the turtles, roll their eyes with glee,
Saying, 'There's no way you swam faster than me!'

Dolphins chuckle at the old whale's sheepish grin,
Reminding him of the days he would win.
'You swam with the currents, but now you've grown slow,

Just hang out with us, and put on a show!'

With each passing wave, memories do glare,
Of fishy romances and underwater fare.
Whale blubbers out a tune, calling for mates,
The others giggle, 'Oh, here comes the great!'

Yet wisdom thunders in the depths so wide,
In laughter and stories, all fish abide.
For in this deep blue, with echoes they blend,
Ancient tales bubble up and never end.

Underwater Relics of Time

Near the reef, there lies a rusty shoe,
A fish now sports it, looking quite new.
Coral reefs cradle a spoon and a fork,
Fish dine in style, that's how they work!

An anchor sits deep, covered in kelp,
The octopus winks, pretending to yelp.
A treasure chest opens, revealing old baubles,
Fish wear shiny jewels, just like in fables.

Starfish steal sunglasses, looking quite cool,
While crabs wear a cape, feeling like fools.
A message in a bottle holds an old joke,
Sardines say, "Oh, what an old croak!"

Time flows like waves, a playful design,
With laughter and artifacts intertwined.
In the ocean's heart, where stories align,
Each relic a giggle, a moment divine!

Murmurs of the Forgotten Shore

On the sandbanks stood a crab,
With a cap and shoes so fab.
He danced and jived with such delight,
Who knew crabs can groove all night?

A rusty bucket claimed to speak,
With fishy tales that made us squeak.
It whispered secrets, oh so bold,
Of mermaids lost and treasures sold.

A seagull squawked, 'I'm quite the bird,'
Demanding fish, with every word.
He flaunted feathers, bright and fine,
Claiming he'd dine on sushi divine!

So gather round the coastal breeze,
Where laughter bubbles with such ease.
Each shell and wave has tales to share,
Of creatures grand, beyond compare.

Salty Stories of Yore

A pirate's ghost with fleeting glee,
Told of treasure beneath the sea.
But after a sip, he'd lose his way,
For rum, not gold, would bright his day!

A clam adorned in flashy bling,
Claimed to be the sea's real king.
He strutted proud, his shell a show,
But lost his grip in the undertow!

Fish gossip spilled like diving lures,
'You see that shark? He's gone for tours!'
Their gossip echoed through the foam,
And left us clapping; we felt at home.

With tales from tides and laughter bright,
Every wave brings sheer delight.
The ocean's quirks, so wild and free,
Remind us all, 'Just let it be!'

Beneath Each Breaking Wave

Beneath the waves, a fish quite spry,
Wore sunglasses and asked me, 'Why?'
'Is it too bright for scales like mine?
Or just the sea's way to dine?'

A dolphin laughed, a jester bold,
With flips and tricks, he broke the mold.
He swam in circles, what a sight,
Claimed he'd outpace the moon tonight!

Starfish looked on with vacant stares,
While seaweed danced, forgetting cares.
In currents deep, we found great fun,
With aqua jokes, we all had won!

So dive, my friends, to ocean's desk,
Where laughter floats without a risk.
Each ripple cradles tales absurd,
In the depths, the jokes are stirred.

Driftwood Diaries

A piece of wood that thought it knew,
Had stories from the ocean's crew.
It spoke of storms and silly fish,
Each word a wave, a wished-for dish!

A bottle bobbed with letters old,
Claiming visions of treasure untold.
But when we read, it was quite the flop,
Just recipes from Grandma's shop!

Barnacles turned into grand sages,
Boasting wisdom through the ages.
They said, 'Just stick, and you'll go far,'
Not knowing we'd steal their bizarre!

So gather driftwood by the beach,
And hear the tales that it will teach.
Each wave that crashes, voice untamed,
Brings laughter forth, and joy acclaimed.

Ghosts of Nautical Dreams

Old sailors whisper soft and low,
As jellyfish dance in the salty flow.
A parrot spins tales of stolen gold,
While crabs form a band, growing ever bold.

The fish wear hats and wave their fins,
Telling secrets of long-lost sins.
A clam recites poetry, quite the fuss,
As octopuses nod, drowning in lust.

Mermaids giggle in bubbly delight,
As seaweed wigs sway in the moonlight.
Caught in a whirlpool of laughter's embrace,
Who knew that the sea had such a face?

Bottles bob with messages laughably grand,
"Help! I'm stuck in a terrible band!"
The sea keeps these secrets, one can only assume,
Among flip-flop dreams in the deep blue gloom.

Reflections in the Brine

A dolphin in shades does a cannonball dive,
Chasing reflections of where he's alive.
The sea is a mirror, but oh, what a jest,
As starfish pranksters hold contests at best.

Waves giggle and tumble, making a play,
With sea cucumbers holding a parade today.
In the midst of the currents, sea turtles roll,
Keeping secrets like a well-hidden shoal.

Fish fashion shows with outfits absurd,
Clams taking selfies, all the weirdest birds.
Anemones blush as they sway with delight,
"Behold our fine fashion, shining so bright!"

But deep down below, in a kelp purple haze,
An old eel stirs, planning pranks in a daze.
His laughter echoes through bubbles and brine,
As currents of fun intertwine through all time.

Fortunes Beneath the Foam

Pirate chests filled with rubber ducks,
Footnote treasures and upside-down luck.
The seagulls squawk about winning the dive,
As mermaid fortune tellers flutter and thrive.

Beneath the foam where sea cucumbers glow,
An iceberg shrugs with a frosty 'hello.'
The tides carry whispers of fishy debates,
Who's the best swimmer, who's got the great traits?

Old boots are the gold they find with great glee,
"Wear these in the water, or swim just like me!"
Jellyfish giggle, their laughter is sly,
In oceans of riches, oh my, oh my!

So dance on the waves with a goofy old tune,
For fortunes of laughter come swiftly, none too soon.
Where bubbles hold secrets, and foam's full of schemes,
The ocean is richer than any of our dreams!

Windswept Histories

The gulls tell stories, spun in the breeze,
Of pirates and birthday cakes meant to tease.
Each whisper a giggle, each gust a shout,
As sea monsters plot how to join the clout.

A lighthouse sways, giving lamps a spin,
Winking as waves toss their wild grins.
A crab with a monocle runs the show,
Holding court over all the salt-infused flow.

The old anchor must be tired, or maybe just cranky,
As wind socks pretend to look all swanky.
Seaglass shards chuckle, reflecting the past,
The tales told by water are sure to last.

So let the breezes tickle your mind,
As you sail through the laughter that history designed.
Raise your glass high, toast to fish that can sing,
For life on the waves is a whimsical fling!

Remnants of Lost Mariner Dreams

A bottle floats with a sock and a shoe,
The sailor wonders, 'What can I do?'
Mermaids giggle, stealing his hat,
While jellyfish dance in a sailor's old spat.

Seagulls squawk tales of treasure and gold,
But all they found was a sandwich grown old.
Fish gossip about ships that once sailed,
With a captain whose pants were forever impaled.

Barnacles stuck to the hull with a grin,
Complain that no one remembers their kin.
Yet under the waves, the laughter does flow,
Of mariners lost in a world full of show.

With every wave, a new joke is told,
Of shipwrecks turned parties, where no one feels cold.
The ocean's a stage, where all things collide,
In a voyage of mirth, where dreams never hide.

Beneath the Surface of Ages

Crabs counsel the fishes over cups made of shells,
Debating the stories of ancient sea jells.
A turtle snaps photos with her smartphone,
While a shark poses, claiming he's the king's clone.

Old bits of driftwood recount ghostly tales,
Of pirates who searched for miraculous snails.
Eels weave in patterns, performing a dance,
As sea cucumbers sigh, 'Give us a chance!'

Octopuses play cards, with eight hands in the game,
Arguing who cheated, but they all feel the same.
The deep's a big laugh, a whimsical maze,
Where even the currents share witty phrases.

In the depths, vibrant bubbles sing loud,
And everybody listens, enraptured, en crowd.
From galleons sunk to barnacle feasts,
The laughter is rich, as it never ceased.

The Ocean's Voice: A Lullaby of Years

The tides murmur songs that tickle your ears,
As whales tell secrets through giggles and cheers.
A clam grins widely, with pearls in its dream,
While dolphins dive deeper, a synchronized team.

Seaweed sways gently, a dance full of grace,
While a crab tries to waltz, but falls on his face.
Seagulls drop snacks from their lofty perch,
Creating a feast with a comical lurch.

Starfish lounge, gossiping endlessly near,
About tourists who wear socks with sandals here.
A conch shell shouts, 'Join in the fun!'
While waves crash and break, full of jest on the run.

Under each ripple, a chuckle remains,
Echoing tales that wind through the lanes.
With naught but a wink, the Ocean's a tease,
Making us smile like it's far too at ease.

Shadows in the Surf

In the foam, shadows flit with mischief in tow,
A crab dons a mask, putting on quite a show.
Seahorses prance, in a synchronized race,
While sea turtles chuckle at their slow pace.

A starfish claims, 'I'm the best swimmer here!'
As barnacles laugh, they refuse to draw near.
Anemones wave like they're hailing a cab,
While jellyfish float by, all dressed to nab.

Bubbles burst forth with a giggly delight,
As fish play charades in the warm, gentle light.
At twilight, the surf holds stories so bright,
Where laughter and waves mingle into the night.

So here on the shore, if you listen real close,
The ocean's strange humor will often propose,
That life beneath waves is a mirthful affair,
Where shadows and laughter float freely on air.

www.ingramcontent.com/pod-product-compliance
Lightning Source LLC
Chambersburg PA
CBHW060142230426
43661CB00003B/535